CANADIAN
WILDLIFE

CANADIAN WILDLIFE

Bruce Obee

Smithbooks

Copyright © 1993 by Bruce Obee
Smithbooks
113 Merton Street
Toronto, Ontario
M4S 1A8

Produced by
Whitecap Books
Vancouver/Toronto

Edited by Elaine Jones
Cover design by Carolyn Deby
Interior design by Betty Skakum
Cover photograph by Thomas Kitchin/First Light

Typeset by CompuType, Vancouver, B.C.

Printed and bound in Canada by D.W. Friesen and Sons Ltd., Altona, Manitoba

Canadian Cataloguing in Publication Data
Obee, Bruce, 1951-
Canadian Wildlife

ISBN 0-88665-220-0

1. Zoology—Canada—Pictorial works. I. Title.
QL219.O23 1993 591.971 C93-091151-2

CONTENTS

INTRODUCTION

Canada, the largest country in the western hemisphere, is among the few remaining places on Earth where true pristine wilderness still exists. Nine-tenths of this nation's 10 million square kilometres are free of human settlement. It is a land of extraordinary landscapes, of impenetrable rain forests, mountains, and slumbrous glaciers, of vast prairie and frozen tundra, of myriad wetlands, oceans and inland waterways.

The wild animals of Canada are as diverse and abundant as the habitats in which they thrive. There are more than 160 species of land mammals, some 520 bird species, 40 amphibians and 42 reptiles. Bounded on three sides by the sea, more than 6.5 million square kilometres of ocean and 243,000 kilometres of coastline lie within Canada's borders. These marine waters are

Canadian caribou, a relative of wild Eurasian reindeer, are northern nomads, travelling as far as twelve hundred kilometres between feeding areas. Large herds wander the northern tundra of Newfoundland, Quebec, the Yukon, and the Northwest Territories.

inhabited by 33 of the world's 85 whale species.

Each of these animals has its own environmental requirements for food, shelter, and reproduction and each occupies its own ecological niche. While some, such as black bears and beavers, mallards and muskrats, occur coast to coast, others, like muskoxen, pronghorn antelope, bison, and rattlesnakes, are found in specific habitats. Some, such as polar bears, cougars, porcupines, and snapping turtles, remain close to home throughout the year. Others are part-time residents who return only to mate or spend summers feeding in Canadian territory: the snow geese, sandpipers, and peregrine falcons of the Arctic are winter citizens of South America; Pacific grey whales that migrate past British Columbia in spring produce their offspring in Baja California; giant Atlantic leatherback turtles travel from the tropics to feed on Nova Scotia jellyfish in summer.

While the image of animals roaming wild and free through the hinterland appeals to the imagination, the wildlife of Canada has not eluded the political bureaucracy that governs our everyday lives. Legally these animals are a publicly owned natural resource, managed, preserved, and harvested under federal and provincial legislation.

Before the advent of formal wildlife management, many of Canada's species suffered severely at the hands of humans. The swift fox, sea mink, great auk, Labrador duck, passenger pigeon, and timber rattlesnake vanished from the country. Today certain populations of cougars, peregrine falcons, plovers, curlews, frogs, turtles, and beluga, bowhead, and right whales are among more than a dozen species that face precarious futures on Canada's endangered-species list.

Before the turn of the century, conservation-minded Canadians

Grey whales were slaughtered to extinction in the Atlantic by the seventeenth century. They nearly suffered a similar fate in the Pacific but were protected when numbers had dwindled to an estimated two thousand. Today about twenty-one thousand grey whales migrate along Canada's Pacific shores.

began to campaign against the unregulated slaughter of the country's wildlife. Immense tracts of wilderness were set aside as national parks, beginning in 1885 in the Rocky Mountains at Banff. But these parks were designed largely to attract tourists, and the public demanded the establishment of wildlife refuges specifically to protect habitat and animals. In 1887 North America's first bird sanctuary was established at Saskatchewan's Last Mountain Lake.

After the National Parks Branch was created in 1911, conservationists began to mobilize across the country: Ducks Unlimited Canada arrived in 1938; the National and Provincial Parks Association was formed in 1963; the Sierra Club of Canada came on the scene in 1970; the Canadian Audubon Society and its affiliates founded the Canadian Nature Federation in 1971; and in 1978 the Committee on the Status of Endangered Wildlife in Canada began to draw up a list of species at risk.

In 1947 the Canadian Wildlife Service was designated to administer the Migratory Birds Convention Act of 1917 in consultation with the ten provinces and two northern territories. The work of the CWS has since expanded to cover mammals and other species, and today more than forty national wildlife areas and eighty nesting sanctuaries have been set aside under the Canada Wildlife Act.

Many modern-day wildlife management principles were conceived in the 1930s by American forester Aldo Leopold, who essentially applied domestic animal husbandry practices to the wild. There are a million hunters in Canada and much of our Canadian wildlife is managed mainly to be harvested.

As we approach the turn of a new century, hunting remains a popular pastime and trapping continues as a source of income

The timber wolf is the largest member of the dog family, weighing as much as forty-five kilograms. Like other predators, it was considered vermin by early settlers. As early as 1793, the Parliament of Upper Canada passed An Act to Encourage the Destruction of Wolves and Bears. The wolf now is found mainly in the north and in some coastal regions.

for many native and non-native Canadians. Traditional attitudes toward our public wildlife resource are changing, however: there's a developing trend toward non-consumptive use of animals. Birding is said to be the fastest-growing outdoor activity on the continent and wildlife viewing has become a priority of government wildlife managers. The value of wild animals merely existing in natural habitats is universally acknowledged. Now, as Canadians stride toward a new century, the future of our wildlife depends upon the lessons we learned from the last.

Canada's Dall's sheep, the only white wild sheep species on Earth, is related to the snow sheep of Siberia. These stocky, powerful mountain dwellers inhabit mountainous regions in the north.

(Overleaf) Snow geese gather in huge flocks during spring and autumn migrations. These Arctic and subarctic breeders lay their eggs on nests built of mud and grass on tussocks. They are particularly abundant in eastern Canada, where a population of about 2.5 million is increasing by some 130,000 a year.

THE PACIFIC COAST

Along the Pacific coast of Canada a wealth of marine life feeds in the plankton-rich waters over the continental shelf. The most productive seas are areas

of coastal upwelling, where the earth's rotation, winds, and local topography force cold, nutrient-laden water up from the depths. In the sunlit surface waters, phytoplankton reproduces by photosynthesis and becomes food for zooplankton. These planktonic plants and animals and the small fish they feed are prey for larger fish, seabirds, whales, dolphins, seals, and sea lions.

Plankton "blooms" under bright summer sunlight, colouring the sea a rusty brown, luring

California sea lions haul out on Race Rocks near Victoria. About thirty-five hundred of these blubbery beasts migrate into southern Canadian waters to spend the winter feeding mainly on herring. Another six thousand larger Steller's sea lions are natives of British Columbia waters.

millions of seabirds and other wildlife to shallow offshore banks. Gulls wheel noisily overhead as they compete for offal discarded from fishboats. Cormorants, murres, pigeon guillemots, loons, and other divers feast on anchovies, herring, and small fish attracted by the plankton.

Whales find food in the same areas. Recent years have seen a notable number of humpback whales returning from their subtropical breeding waters to summer feeding grounds off the Canadian coast. Hunted to near extinction, these graceful behemoths virtually vanished from British Columbia. Now the same whales are appearing in the same areas with encouraging consistency.

It is hoped the humpback's recovery will be as successful as that of the Pacific grey whale which, like the humpback, was slaughtered relentlessly by nineteenth- and twentieth-century whalers. Now about twenty-one thousand grey whales migrate past the B.C. coast every spring and autumn as they travel between Mexican mating lagoons and summer feeding waters in the Bering and Chukchi seas.

These big baleen whales feed on plankton and small fish, while smaller toothed killer whales eat salmon and other marine mammals, including whales larger than themselves. Like other marine life, they are most conspicuous during summer plankton blooms, when migrating salmon take their last meals before homing in to rivers of their birth. And like humpbacks and greys, orca populations are increasing in the Canadian Pacific.

Orcas are the largest members of the dolphin family in the North Pacific. Their smaller black and white relatives, Dall's porpoises, are occasionally mistaken for killer whales. Even smaller are harbour porpoises, a species found on both the Pacific and Atlantic coasts. In recent

The whiskery snout of a sea otter rises above the surface. These clown-like sea mammals were extirpated from Canadian waters in the early 1920s. A total of eighty-nine introduced from Alaska in the late 1960s and early '70s have grown to an estimated eight hundred today.

years, schools of Pacific white-sided dolphins, numbering in the hundreds, have been seen in B.C.'s near-shore waters during summer. Other dolphins occasionally found in Canada's Pacific waters include false killer whales, pilot whales, and Risso's dolphins.

Though most dolphins are seen during summer, a few are observed in winter, a time when Steller's and California sea lions congregate near huge schools of herring. It's not uncommon to see as many as two thousand sea lions, burping and barking as they hang about islets, reefs, floats, and log booms, gorging themselves on herring that hold in sheltered bays while maturing to spawn. These sea lions are invariably surrounded by enormous flocks of seabirds numbering in the thousands, tens of thousands, and occasionally in the hundreds of thousands.

An animal seldom seen in Pacific waters is the fuzzy-faced sea otter. Extirpated from Canada in the 1920s, populations building along the west coast today were introduced from Alaska in the late 1960s and early '70s. They inhabit reef-ridden, surf-battered offshore kelp beds, feeding on red sea urchins and shellfish.

The mild, Mediterranean-type climate of the Pacific coast is unique in Canada. Abundant food and ice-free waters attract a variety of wintering birds from waterfowl to passerines. These birds, along with herring and spawning salmon, are prey for bald eagles that migrate from interior nesting sites. It is estimated that between twenty thousand and thirty thousand bald eagles winter on Canada's west coast.

The ocean is joined to the mountains that flank the coastline by countless spawning streams. Salmon that feed offshore become food for terrestrial animals—grizzly and black bears, otters, mink, raccoons, and others that stalk the river-

Though plentiful on Canada's Pacific coast, the elusive timber wolf is rarely seen by people. Deer and small mammals are its prime prey, but wolf tracks are occasionally seen on beaches, where it has been known to forage for fish and crustaceans in tide pools.

banks. Even timber wolves have been known to take spawning salmon.

One rarely observed animal is the pure white kermode bear, a black-bear subspecies exclusive to a small part of B.C.'s northwest coast. It has, at times, been mistaken for a misplaced polar bear. Early kermode observers claimed it was an albino black bear, but its brown eyes dismissed that theory.

Another elusive, yet plentiful, species is the cougar. This fifty-kilogram cat takes a variety of prey—mice, bear cubs, raccoons, otters. On the coast it relies mainly on blacktail deer. Each year a few cougars meander through residential areas, dining on unfortunate family pets.

Common murres, gulls, and cormorants share a roost on the Pacific coast. Literally millions of seabirds feed on schooling fish and other marine life in plankton-rich eddies and upwellings off the continental shelf. About 6 million seabirds breed on Canada's Pacific coast and another 40 million mate in neighbouring Alaska.

(Overleaf) Humpback whales, hunted to near extinction in the Pacific, are being seen with increasing frequency off Canadian shores. These gentle giants may grow to thirty-five tonnes by feeding on minuscule planktonic organisms and small schooling fish.

(Above) Harbour seals, numbering as many as a hundred thousand in the Canadian Pacific, are the most commonly seen marine mammal. Populations have been growing by about 12 percent a year since they were protected in 1970.

(Opposite) Little is known of the white kermode bear, a black-bear subspecies that inhabits only a small area on the north coast of British Columbia. Known as the snow bear, it has been mistaken for a misplaced polar bear.

(Above) The common loon is one of four loon species found on Canada's west coast. This species, with its contrasting black and white summer plumage, is the one most often depicted in the art of coastal natives.

(Opposite) A male grizzly may weigh four hundred kilograms and stand upright at more than three metres. When lumbering along on its massive forelegs, the top of its distinctive hump may be more than a metre from the ground. One forepaw, which could measure twenty centimetres across the palm, is well over twice the size of a human hand. About thirty-five hundred wander the watersheds of Canada's Pacific coast.

The Steller's jay, a robin-sized, iridescent blue freebooter, shamelessly pilfers unguarded food at picnic tables and campsites. The only crested jay in the west, the Steller's was adopted as British Columbia's provincial bird in 1987.

(Above) The raccoon, which inhabits nearly all of southern Canada, is a proficient beachcomber, feeding on snails, crabs, and small fish caught from tide pools. Raccoons are also downtown wildlife, overturning garbage cans and raiding composts and pet bowls in residential areas. Though it may weigh only eight kilograms, the raccoon is a formidable adversary if cornered.

(Overleaf) A bald eagle tends its eaglets in a lofty stick nest. The number of eagles that breed on the Pacific coast is unknown, but winter counts show that between twenty thousand and thirty thousand inhabit Canada's west coast in the nonbreeding season. Lured by mild temperatures, abundant waterfowl, herring and spawning salmon, these stately raptors migrate to the coast from Alaska, Montana, Idaho, Oregon, Washington, and the interior of British Columbia.

Blacktail fawns enjoy freedom from hunters in Canada's Gulf Islands.
Blacktails, slightly smaller than whitetail deer, are a coastal species
and the major quarry of wolves and cougars. Their dense fur helps keep
them afloat as they swim between islands and across coastal inlets.

The cougar, Canada's largest wildcat, may measure three metres from nose to tail and weigh fifty kilograms. It can take an elk or moose three times its size. On the Pacific coast, its range varies in elevation with movements of blacktail deer. Cougar tracks on remote beaches are seen occasionally, but cougars, like wolves, are seldom sighted.

(Above) The river otter, unlike its closest cousin the sea otter, is one of the most abundant seashore mammals on the west coast. Though its fur is inferior to that of the sea otter, the river otter was also hunted by early traders and remains the legal prey of today's fur trappers. At fourteen kilos, a full-grown river otter is about half the size of a sea otter.

(Opposite) The black-capped chickadee is an endearing little bird, always appearing cheerful as it busily forages for insects, seeds, and wild fruit. It is easily attracted to bird feeders and will allow people to approach within a metre or two. On the nest the female wards off intruders with a sudden snakelike hiss.

The dorsal fin of an orca, or killer whale, may stand as high as two metres on a big bull. Slightly more than four hundred orcas that have been identified through photographs are seen regularly on the Pacific coast. In recent years groups of thirty and forty unidentified orcas have been spotted off the west coast of Vancouver Island and the Queen Charlotte Islands.

The black bear is Canada's smallest and most common bear. A large boar may weigh two hundred kilos, about half as much as a grizzly. They are common in Pacific watersheds, where their seasonal wanderings take them from alpine meadows to surf-battered beaches.

THE CANADIAN ARCTIC

The wildlife of the Canadian Arctic has evolved to endure the world's most inhospitable climate. It is a bleak, treeless terrain where a temperature of -12°C drops 20 degrees in a forty-kilometre wind. Through the long months of winter the sun never dawns in the high Arctic and 10°C is considered a warm summer day.

The animals here adapt to these harsh conditions in various ways. Polar bears and muskoxen are cloaked in heavy fur and minimize wind chill by carrying their massive forms close to the ground on short legs. Arctic foxes are followed by long, fluffy tails to wrap their bodies for warmth when they curl up to

Barren-ground caribou, the great migrators of the tundra, may move fifty kilometres a day. Herds numbering in the thousands travel across the Arctic barrens on trails established centuries ago. Both cows and bulls grow antlers that are shed in late fall or early winter.

sleep in drifting snow. The legs of ptarmigan and snowy owls are covered with feathers. Ducks and geese have layers of fat and short, feltlike down beneath their feathers. Seals, whales, and walruses are protected from frigid seas and pack ice by thick blubber. Noses, ears, and tails of some species are short, leaving less area exposed to the elements.

With much of the ground covered in snow and ice most of the year, some animals have special foot gear. The Arctic wolf grows tufts of stiff hair between its foot pads to fend off the cold. The collared lemming produces sharp winter claws for scurrying over ice, and the muskox has hooves designed for travel over slippery surfaces.

Unable to dig in the permafrost to hibernate, many Arctic animals must hunt year round and camouflage is important to both predator and prey. Polar bears, Arctic foxes and wolves, snowy owls, gyrfalcons, ermine,

ptarmigan, and Arctic hares all dress in snow white to blend with their surroundings. The ground squirrel is the only Arctic animal to hibernate, digging beneath the surface snow. While sleeping, its body temperature drops to near freezing, lowering its pulse to about three heartbeats per minute.

Hundreds of thousands of nesting birds avoid Arctic winters by simply flying somewhere else. Gulls, terns, shorebirds, loons, larks, sparrows, geese, ducks, and swans spend a few short summer weeks at these high latitudes before migrating south. While some travel only as far as the southern Prairies or the Pacific or Atlantic coasts, others move great distances. Herring gulls winter on the beaches of southern California; Baird's and buff-breasted sandpipers fly to South America.

Ironically, birds that escape formidable Arctic winters by migrating to warmer climes sometimes face other perils.

Long wavy lines of snow geese in flight are easily identified by the black wing tips. Counts taken at Cap Tourmente National Wildlife Area near Quebec City, where hundreds of thousands stop each year, show significant increases in snow goose numbers during this century. Snow geese from the Canadian Arctic winter in Mexico and the southern United States.

Snow geese that hatch in the Canadian Arctic are shot by Texas waterfowl hunters. Peregrine falcons that nest in the Canadian north are officially endangered, not because of harsh Arctic conditions, but because of DDT and other pesticides that contaminate their prey in South American wintering grounds.

Some year-round Arctic animals live on neither land nor sea. Polar bears spend most of their time wandering the pack ice in search of surfacing seals. They are shadowed by Arctic foxes that feed on carrion left by the bears. Ringed seals and ivory gulls move onto the ice to raise their young. Other ocean-going animals, such as walruses and murres, move from the sea onto land to breed.

Above the shores the boundless tundra stretches across the Canadian Arctic. Great herds of barren-ground caribou stop to feed here between extensive, and intensive, spring and autumn migrations. Unlike its closest relative, the Peary caribou does not travel in massive herds, but in groups of three or four, foraging for grasses, flowers, lichens, sedges, and shrubs. Also unlike the barren-ground caribou, the near-white Peary caribou is on the endangered-species list. This subspecies is particularly susceptible to inclement weather, and major die-offs have occurred naturally.

The Peary caribou shares its endangered status with three other Arctic species. The Eskimo curlew, once numbering in the millions, was hunted relentlessly in the Arctic, while its southern winter habitats were alienated for agriculture. No one is sure if any even exist today. In the ocean, the belugas of southeast Baffin Island and the eastern Arctic population of bowhead whales have been reduced to worrisome levels.

(Opposite) This immature Arctic hare will grow to the size of a cat and become prey for predators. Stiff bristles of hair grow between its toes, enabling it to travel across snow.

(Overleaf) Unlike hibernating bears, the restless polar bears of the Arctic remain active through winter, when they wander the pack ice, waiting by breathing holes for surfacing seals. When the ice breaks up in summer they are often forced ashore to feed.

(Above) The white Peary caribou, known as the ghost of the tundra, is the smallest and most northerly of Canada's Arctic caribou. It is susceptible to harsh winters, when large die-offs have occurred, and is officially listed as threatened in Canada.

(Opposite) The great horned owl, with its prominent ear tufts, bright yellow eyes, and white throat, is widely distributed across North America. At about fifty-five centimetres high, it is one of the largest owls. In the Arctic its plumage is lighter than in southern areas. When snowshoe hare populations drop, great horned owls disperse from their Arctic territories and turn to other prey.

(Above) The sixty-centimetre gyrfalcon is the world's largest falcon. Plumage varies from brownish gray to white with black back stripes. In the Canadian Arctic the gyrfalcon feeds largely on ptarmigan and breeds across the tundra from the Yukon to Labrador.

(Opposite) The ivory tusks of the walrus are more than mere decoration. Up to thirty-six centimetres long, the tusks are used to punch breathing holes in the ice and to haul its bulky body onto ice floes. Its sensitive, quill-like whiskers detect bivalves and molluscs, which it digs up with its tusks. These massive mammals, often weighing nearly a tonne, are found in Canada's eastern Arctic.

Red-throated loons breeding in the Arctic carry out elaborate
courtship displays in which they repeatedly dip their bills and rush one
another underwater. Almost as large as a Canada goose, the red-
throated loon is usually seen alone or in pairs. It gathers in large
flocks where food is plentiful. After breeding in the Arctic, it disperses
along both coasts of the continent as far south as Mexico.

(Above) The grinning face of a beluga whale surfaces in the cold Arctic sea. This toothed whale, related to dolphins and porpoises, is plentiful in the Arctic but is endangered in some areas. Northern natives continue to hunt belugas for oil and skins.

(Overleaf) The muskox's long, shaggy mane was almost the cause of its demise. In the late 1800s and early 1900s more than fifteen thousand Canadian muskox hides were used for sleigh rugs. The muskox sheds about three kilos of qiviut each summer.

The pigeon-sized white-tailed ptarmigan is camouflaged from enemies by pure white plumage. This tundra nester grows long claws and thick tufts of feathers on both sides of its feet to walk on snow. This special foot gear reduces the distance the foot sinks in the snow by half and increases the bearing surface of the foot by about 400 percent.

Immature snowy owls carry dark bars in their plumage before turning pure white or white with scattered dark marks. After an elaborate courtship, which includes the male dancing rigidly with a lemming in its mouth, a pair makes a grass-lined depression in the ground and nests on the open tundra. Clutch size and breeding frequency are closely tied to the availability of lemmings. When lemmings are scarce, snowy owls may migrate as far south as the northern United States.

(Above) At the end of each breeding season, the Arctic terns of Canada's most northerly latitudes may migrate as far as the southern tip of South America or Antarctica, a one-way distance of eighteen thousand kilometres. This slender, black-capped seabird vigorously defends its nest, attacking any intruders, including humans, who venture too close.

(Opposite) Stooping at speeds of more than three hundred kilometres an hour, the peregrine falcon is likely North America's fastest bird. Peregrines have been severely affected by DDT and other pesticides as well as dwindling nesting habitat. The peregrines of the Arctic are officially listed as threatened.

Arctic foxes are able to detect the scent of their preferred prey—
lemmings—through the snow. They also feed on other rodents, birds,
fish, and shellfish and will follow polar bears and wolves to scavenge
leftover carcasses. These foxes shed their thick white winter fur and
don lighter brown coats in summer.

A willow ptarmigan is difficult to see against a backdrop of Arctic willow. In winter its plumage turns white. Like the rock and white-tailed ptarmigan, this northern breeder defends its offspring by distracting intruders while the chicks hide in the bush.

The siksik, or Arctic ground squirrel, is the far north's only true hibernator, sleeping about seven months of the year. Its burrows, nearly a metre underground, may consist of individual tunnels up to eighteen metres long with as many as fifty entrances.

*The long-tailed jaeger is the smallest of Canada's three jaeger
species. A slender, ternlike bird, the jaeger's long, divided tail
distinguishes it from similar seabirds. While nesting in the Arctic, it
competes with other predators for lemmings, smaller birds, insects,
and fish. It winters as far south as Ecuador and Chile.*

THE ROCKY MOUNTAINS

Four thousand kilometres from the Atlantic and only seven hundred from the Pacific, the Rocky Mountains split the nation into east and west. Here on the Great Continental Divide, the Columbia Icefield is the birthplace of Canada's mightiest

rivers: the Fraser, running a convoluted course over British Columbia to the Pacific; the Saskatchewan, flowing across the Prairies, through Lake Winnipeg into Hudson Bay; the Athabasca, running northeast to swell the waters of the Mackenzie River and drain into the Arctic Ocean.

This Rocky Mountain dividing point is the interior edge of the western Cordillera, one of the

Bighorn sheep of the Rockies may stand higher than a metre at the shoulder and weigh up to 155 kilograms. Each year another ring grows on their heavy horns. Old sheep often lose the tips of their horns during mating rivalry. These gregarious ungulates migrate up and down the slopes in small bands, changing elevations with the snow.

world's major mountain systems, a significant influence on the distribution of wildlife throughout much of the country. These mountains are a predominant factor in climatic differences between east and west, sheltering the low-lying Prairies from moisture-laden Pacific weather systems. It is a region of divergent landscapes with valley bottoms and peaks ranging from one thousand to four thousand metres, creating an assortment of microclimates and habitats from coniferous forests and wetlands to steep talus, open meadows, and alpine tundra.

The varied habitats here are home to Canada's greatest diversity of wildlife species, from the minuscule pygmy shrew to the lordly moose. Much of the habitat is protected within Canada's four Rocky Mountain national parks—Banff, Jasper, Kootenay, and Yoho—where travellers often catch roadside glimpses of black bears, chipmunks, squirrels, and grazing elk or wapiti. People who stop to scan the scree and greenery above the highways occasionally spot mountain goats and Rocky Mountain bighorn sheep nibbling the grasses above the treeline. While goats prefer open alpine throughout the year, bighorn sheep are seen most often in spring and summer, feeding on meadows between forests, always within easy reach of steep and rocky escape terrain.

Black bears like similar areas in spring when fresh grass, angelica, sweet cicely, horsetail, clover, cow parsnip, and dandelions emerge from their winter dormancy. Later, summer berries attract black bears and grizzlies. Both bears are mainly vegetarians but will feed on meat and carrion when opportunities arise. In the alpine the grizzly is a tireless digger, unearthing pocket gophers, pikas, and the odd hoary or yellow-bellied marmot from their burrows. In the valley bottoms the grizzly is an

A moose, the world's largest deer, takes a break from browsing on twigs in the Rockies. An eight-hundred-kilo bull may devour more than twenty kilograms of twigs a day. These lordly loners prefer meadows, bogs, lake edges, and burned forests in subalpine regions.

adept fisher, catching salmon in its teeth or herding them into shallows as they head upstream to spawn. Recent studies suggest as many as two thousand grizzlies may roam the Canadian Rockies. Summer hikers occasionally become grizzly-bear prey.

Autumn hikers are often startled by a peculiar, high-pitched whistle resounding through the mountains. During the fall rut, wapiti, Canada's most vocal deer, bugle into the sunset, challenging other bulls for mates. Like other ungulates of the Rockies—caribou, moose, whitetail, and mule deer—wapiti often fall victim to wolves and cougars. Both of these carnivores are proficient predators but, unlike their prey, are rarely seen. Their cousins, coyotes and bobcats, feed on rodents and birds and are more commonly spotted by Rocky Mountain explorers. The lynx, the bobcat's larger kin, is more like the cougar in its secretive ways. It is not as versatile a feeder as the bobcat, relying almost exclusively on the snowshoe hare.

The highlands and forests of the Rockies are inhabited by numerous bird species, including grouse, ptarmigan, pheasants, partridges, sapsuckers, woodpeckers, and jays. The lower elevations are home to ducks and geese, coots, swans, buffleheads, blackbirds, dippers, kingfishers, and more. Many of these birds, along with a multitude of rodents, are fair game for owls, hawks and falcons, ospreys and eagles.

Besides the birds, bears, and bigger species, the Rockies support a variety of smaller mammals, such as weasels, spotted and striped skunks, badgers, pine martens, fishers, wolverines, river otters, woodchucks, porcupines, and bats. A familiar sound to alpine hikers is the high-pitched warning whistle of the hoary marmot.

(Opposite) The large feet and talons of the osprey, which feeds on fish, are covered near the ends with sharp spicules that help grip its prey. Often called fish hawks, ospreys hover at a height of ten to thirty metres before diving into the water.

(Overleaf) The sure-footed mountain goat is equipped with skidproof soles on its hooves to grip steep rock slopes. Despite its specialized feet, a few mountain goats plunge to their deaths each year.

A ten-point whitetail buck is distracted from its grazing in a high-elevation meadow. A keen sense of smell and acute hearing alert white-tails to predators, such as cougars and wolves. Whitetails can escape through a forest at speeds of fifty kilometres an hour. In the Rockies this species inhabits woodlands, forested riverbanks, and swamp edges.

The long-legged lynx is a nocturnal predator relying heavily on the snowshoe hare. When hare populations crash, lynx numbers decline shortly after. Though fast and agile, the lynx succeeds in only 15 percent of its attacks.

Clark's nutcrackers breed at high elevations in the Rockies while deep snow is still on the ground. These jaylike birds can carry nearly a hundred conifer seeds in sublingual pouches. They may stash as many as thirty thousand seeds and remember the locations of a thousand caches.

Of the Rockies' three wildcat species—bobcat, lynx, and cougar—the bobcat is most likely to be seen. Slightly smaller than the lynx, it wanders canyons and valleys stalking rodents and birds. It is an adept climber and often feeds on birds' eggs.

(Above) Adult hoary marmots, weighing up to six kilograms, are the largest members of the squirrel family. Known as whistlers, their shrill alarms warn other mountain dwellers of impending danger. They live in alpine colonies, burrowing under boulders for protection from predators such as grizzly bears.

(Opposite) Young red squirrels peer out from a nest in a hollow tree. These chattery rodents are common in the forests of the Rockies, where they retreat to the treetops and loudly scold those who invade their territories. They spend much of their summers stockpiling seeds, nuts, and fungi to eat through winter.

(Above) Although the marten hunts mainly on the ground, it is a nimble climber. It is known to skydive from coniferous trees, landing ten or twelve metres from the trunk. Martens are secretive animals, rarely seen by people except when caught in traps.

(Opposite) The porcupine protects its body with thirty thousand needle-sharp quills. Loosely attached to the porcupine's skin, they gather like burrs on any animal that touches them. Though it would rather run than fight, it can deliver fifty or a hundred quills with a single swat of its tail.

A hamster-sized pika blends with the boulders of its grassy meadow.
These rock rabbits build miniature haystacks of dried vegetation to eat
through winter when they take shelter beneath the mountain snow.
They jealously guard their haystacks, kicking out trespassers with
their hind feet or boxing them with their forepaws.

(Above) As many as two thousand grizzlies may roam the Canadian Rockies. While hikers in the country's four Rocky Mountain national parks are attacked occasionally by grizzlies, the species' reputation as a ferocious killer is unjust. Grizzlies are omnivorous, feeding far more on vegetation than on other animals. They do, however, unearth ground squirrels and other rodents from their burrows, and during spawning season they test their piscatory skills in mountain streams.

(Overleaf) The caribou of the Rockies inhabit higher elevations than their Arctic kin and may migrate only a few kilometres in small groups. When pursued by wolves or other predators, they are able to run seventy or eighty kilometres an hour, seeking refuge in the woods.

(Above) The wily coyote, like the red fox, is widespread but not abundant in the Rocky Mountains. Feeding on rodents, birds, and insects, a full-grown coyote may weigh thirteen kilograms, about a third as much as a wolf. Like wolves, they often hunt in family packs.

(Opposite) Wapiti, or American elk, Canada's most vocal deer, bugle across the valleys of the Rockies just before sunset, emitting high-pitched whistles. Their impressive, twelve-point antlers are tipped with ivory and were once used to make handles for cutlery. In the Rocky Mountain towns of Banff and Jasper, it's not uncommon for a friendly wapiti to peer inside a house, leaving a noseprint on the window.

(Above) Wood duck drakes in full summer plumage adorn a mountain pond. Carvers, painters, and photographers have devoted entire careers to immortalizing this bird's resplendent beauty. These dazzling ducks raise their offspring in cavities in deciduous trees before migrating to the southern states and Mexico for winter.

(Opposite) The snowshoe hare is nicknamed the varying hare because of its seasonal changes in colour. This brown hare turns snow white in winter. The biological cycles of snowshoe hares are extreme, peaking and collapsing every eight to twelve years. The cycles of predators, such as coyotes, lynx, great horned owls, red foxes, and goshawks, are closely tied to that of the snowshoe hare.

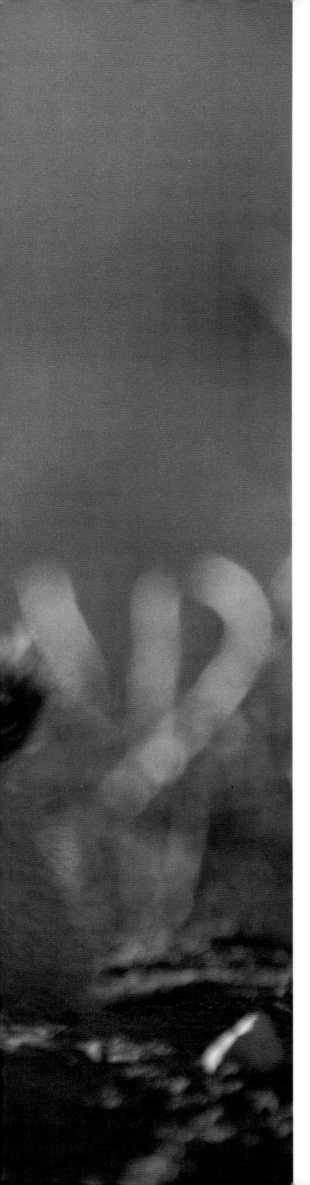

THE PRAIRIES

Canadian wildlife conservation had its beginning in the Prairies. It was here in 1887, at the north end of Last Mountain Lake, eighty kilometres north of Regina, that the first bird sanctuary on the continent was established. More than a century later the four-square-kilometre sanctuary remains a haven for migrating waterfowl and other birds, including whooping cranes and Ross's geese. In mid-September as many as twenty thousand sandhill cranes and ten thousand double-crested cormorants stop here. White-winged scoters and white pelicans nest on islands in the lake and sharp-tailed grouse, common terns, American avocets, mallards, and more nest

A black-tailed prairie dog suns itself outside its burrow. These tubby rodents emerge from their underground lairs shortly after sunrise to feed and socialize with other residents of the dog town. Their intricate subterranean warrens may be as deep as two metres below the surface and run a horizontal distance of twelve metres.

elsewhere around the shores.

More than 70 percent of North America's waterfowl breed on the Canadian Prairies. As early as 1938 the private conservation group Ducks Unlimited recognized the importance of these vast wetlands and launched its first enhancement project at Big Grass Marsh, 120 kilometres northwest of Winnipeg. Since then Ducks Unlimited has spent nearly $300 million on some three thousand wetland projects involving 1.5 million hectares in Canada, mainly on the Prairies.

In keeping with conservation tradition, in 1988 the Quill Lakes, thirty-five kilometres northeast of Last Mountain Lake, were chosen for Canada's first preservation project under the North American Waterfowl Management Plan. This 1986 Canada-U.S. agreement is an effort to protect and improve 1.5 million hectares of waterfowl habitat by the turn of the century.

The countless pothole lakes and sloughs across the great plains of Alberta, Saskatchewan, and Manitoba encompass about 750,000 square kilometres of prime waterfowl habitat. They are a muddy mix of rich plant and animal life, teeming with insects, molluscs, crustaceans and amphibians that sustain a plethora of birds. In Manitoba alone some 340 of Canada's 500-odd bird species occur. Delta Marsh, twenty-five kilometres north of Portage la Prairie, is an internationally known nesting region for redheads, canvasbacks, shovelers, green- and blue-winged teals, pintails, scaups, ring-necked ducks, and mallards; it is also a stopover for white pelicans and trumpeter swans. The Minnedosa Potholes area, ninety kilometres west of Lake Manitoba, is among the most productive waterfowl breeding areas on the Prairies.

But the Prairies are not all ducks and waterbirds. The waterfowl, along with rodents, are the quarry of several rap-

The yellow-shafted flicker lives in woodlands east of the Rocky Mountains. It occasionally eats seeds, nuts, and grains, but survives mainly on ants and other insects, feeding on the ground more than any other woodpecker. It usually nests in tree cavities, which it often excavates itself.

torial birds, including sharp-shinned hawks, great grey owls, and bald eagles. One of the most interesting is the threatened burrowing owl. This long-legged, robin-sized raptor is often seen standing on fence posts. In winter its habitat is invaded by the pure white snowy owl, a summer resident of the Arctic.

In 1981 more than nine hundred square kilometres of grasslands were preserved in southwest Saskatchewan with the creation of Grasslands National Park. The park is a refuge for coyotes, red foxes, and mule deer. It is also an asylum for about six thousand black-tailed prairie dogs, gregarious gopher-like rodents that once built "dog towns" from Saskatchewan to Texas. Like other Prairie wildlife, they were eliminated from most of their territory by ranchers and farmers.

Perhaps the most familiar Prairie rodent is the ubiquitous northern pocket gopher, a smaller cousin of the prairie dog. The mounds of this busy burrower are scattered across the grasslands from the Rockies to southwestern Manitoba. Except during spring mating season, the gopher is a solitary animal, spending from August to October tunnelling and gathering roots for winter storage. Its intricate underground warren may lie two or three metres below the surface. Like the prairie dog, the gopher's digging and foraging habits damage gardens and grain fields, making it a prime target for disgruntled farmers.

Another animal that suffered severely at the hands of agriculturists is the pronghorn antelope, the only member of the antelope family left in North America. In the early 1900s three national sanctuaries were established in the southern Prairies to rebuild pronghorn populations that were losing habitat to farmers. So successful was their comeback that in 1947 the sanctuaries were abolished

Burrowing owls take over abandoned burrows of prairie dogs and ground squirrels on open grasslands, golf courses, or airports. They line their nests with cow and horse dung, dry grass, pellets, and feathers. When threatened in their burrows, they mimic the rattle of a rattlesnake.

as unnecessary.

The bison of the great plains, however, were not so fortunate. These burly beasts numbered about 50 or 60 million in the early 1800s, providing food for wolves, grizzlies, scavengers, Indians, and Métis. Herds of wood bison numbering in the thousands grazed the lowland meadows and deltas of the Slave, Peace, and Athabasca rivers. Other regions were occupied by great herds of larger plains bison.

Slaughter of these animals after the arrival of European settlers reduced both bison subspecies to near-extinction by 1885. They were protected under Canadian law in 1894. Thirteen years later the government bought some plains bison from Yellowstone National Park in the U.S. and established a herd near Wainright, Alberta. In 1922 Wood Buffalo National Park, a 44,840-square-kilometre refuge on the Alberta-Northwest Territories border, was set aside to salvage North America's last herd of wood bison, about fifteen hundred animals.

In 1925 nearly sixty-seven hundred plains bison were transferred to the park from Wainright. Crossbreeding produced a hybridization that almost wiped out the wood bison as a distinct subspecies. Fortunately, in 1975, a remnant population of pure wood bison was located in the park and some were moved to Elk Island National Park, near Edmonton, and to the north shore of Great Slave Lake, where their survival has been good.

(Above) In spring, amorous sage grouse move onto Prairie leks, or courtship grounds, to impress potential mates with their flamboyant courtship displays. They strut across the grasslands with neck sacs inflated, tails fanned, and wings held rigid. They throw back their heads and deflate their neck sacs with a loud cracking sound.

(Overleaf) Pronghorn antelopes are common in southern Alberta and Saskatchewan, gathering in herds of a hundred or so in winter. During spring they break into groups of five or ten. Mature males engage in shoving matches as they gather harems of a dozen-odd does. Pronghorns, unlike other deer, refuse to jump fences and other obstacles which impede their migratory movements.

A great horned owl tends its young in a large stick nest. It's common for this species to take over nests abandoned by other raptors. Like other owls, it hunts mainly at night. An extremely acute sense of sight and hearing, wings specially designed for silent flight, and familiarity with its territory combine to make for successful hunting.

*Red foxes have become so widespread during this century that
competition for space with others of its species is a major source of
stress. Though uncommon on the southern plains, they are abundant in
the north, where they defend territories vehemently, often inflicting
serious injuries.*

(Above) As tall as a five-year-old child, the sandhill crane is distinguished from other large wading birds by the bare red patch on its crown. They travel in large, noisy flocks, issuing loud, hollow calls that can be heard for two kilometres. In mid-September as many as twenty thousand pass through Saskatchewan's Last Mountain Lake Bird Sanctuary.

(Opposite) The thirteen-lined ground squirrel is a loner among the half-dozen ground squirrels of western Canada. Unlike the others, which excavate tunnels with conspicuous entrances on open grasslands, it prefers overgrown fields and shrubbery, where it digs shallow burrows with well-hidden openings.

(Above) The green-winged teal is the smallest dabbling duck, flying in swiftly moving groups that turn and twist like shorebird flocks. It occupies shallow marshes, ponds, grain fields, and mud flats, where it scuttles about in search of seeds. A female feigns injury to defend its young, which hide in nearby bush.

(Opposite) For most of this century the whooping crane has teetered on the edge of extinction, a victim of hunting and the drainage of wetlands for agriculture. In 1941 there were fewer than two dozen left in North America. Under a Canada-U.S. program, eggs are hatched and young are raised in captivity, using sandhill cranes as foster parents. They are slow to reproduce, however, and today there may be fewer than two hundred whooping cranes.

The white back and tail feathers of a canvasback are marked by waves of fine dusky lines. It lays its eggs in concealed, basket-shaped nests of vegetation over water. Occasionally it moves into an abandoned muskrat lodge. This bird is often the victim of the American coot, which pirates aquatic vegetation foraged by the canvasback.

(Above) Bison, which once ranged across the Prairies in the millions, were reduced nearly to extinction before they were protected in 1894. Through conservation programs, herds have been established in Canada at Wainright, Great Slave Lake, and Elk Island and Wood Buffalo national parks.

(Overleaf) Mule deer, a close relative of whitetail deer, browse on short plants and brush at forest edges. Known as jumping deer, muleys leap over high obstacles and run erratic courses to escape enemies. Mule deer are plentiful on the Prairies and appear to be expanding their range northward.

Canada's six garter-snake species are among thirty types of garter snakes occurring from the Northwest Territories to Costa Rica. They are harmless to humans, helping control slugs, bugs, and other garden pests.

The yellow-headed blackbird is a marshland yodeler, singing a discordant song from its perch atop shoreside vegetation. Its basketlike nest hangs amid reeds and bullrushes in marshes, sloughs, and shallow lakes.

White pelicans near Riding Mountain National Park in southwestern Manitoba are among more than 230 bird species found in the park. These big birds may measure 160 centimetres from head to tail. They catch crayfish, salamanders, and small fish by dipping their heavy bills and heads underwater.

The redpoll, distinguished from most other finches by its red crown patch, is surprisingly tame and can be easily approached. Flocks of redpolls have established hierarchies, with females dominating males during nesting and roles reversing between breeding seasons.

EASTERN CANADA

East of the Prairies the myriad lakes and waterways of the Canadian Shield extend across most of Ontario and Quebec. This broad band of plateaus and highlands arcs around the coasts of Hudson and James bays, giving way to the Hudson Bay Lowland

in the north. In the south the shield slopes toward the shores of the Great Lakes.

Marshes here are extensive, dominating much of the land around Lakes St. Clair, Huron, and Ontario, and near the upper St. Lawrence River. One of the most expansive is the eighty-one-hundred-hectare Minesing Swamp, near Peterborough. People who walk the four-hundred-kilometre Ganaraska Trail,

A beaver tows a freshly cut willow switch across a placid pond. The lush fur of Canada's biggest rodent was largely responsible for the exploration and settlement of the nation. The beaver remains an important fur-bearing animal and today is honoured in more than a thousand Canadian place names.

which skirts the swamp, may see snapping turtles, star-nosed moles, muskrats, and 160 summer bird species.

The streams, lakes, bogs, and muskeg of this region support a profusion of wildlife, from bears, birds, and beavers to rattlesnakes and snapping turtles. The fur-bearing animals of the Canadian Shield—beavers, weasels, fishers, foxes, lynx, martens, mink, muskrats, otters, wolverines, and others—played a pivotal part in the early exploration and economic development of Canada. Like the nomadic Algonquian hunters before them, European fur traders used birchbark canoes to traverse this difficult terrain and penetrate deep into the heart of Canada.

The most valuable of these animals was the ubiquitous beaver, whose underfur was used to make felt hats, a symbol of prestige in Europe during the eighteenth and nineteenth centuries. From the Maritimes to the Pacific, fur traders bartered with native Indians for the pelts. The beaver, North America's largest rodent, was almost extinguished, but after the 1830s, when silk hats became fashionable in Europe, demand for beaver fur decreased. The species rebounded so successfully that in 1946 Canadian beavers were introduced to the southern end of South America, where there now is a thriving population.

In Canada today this indefatigable bog logger bustles about slow-flowing streams in aspen and willow groves, building its dams and lodges, enjoying its eminence as the country's national emblem. The beaver now is honoured in more than a thousand place names across Canada. The beaver is still important to the fur industry; trappers within the past decade have killed nearly half a million Canadian beavers during some years.

The beaver shares its marshy habitat with an assortment of aquatic animals. Many of

Early trappers believed this animal's bold theft of bait and victims from their traps was the work of the devil. At about twenty kilos, the wolverine is one of the largest members of the weasel family. It is a powerful animal, with jaws capable of crushing bones and chewing through frozen meat.

Red-winged blackbirds are among the more attractive species, visually and vocally, found in meadows, marshes, and wet fields. These birds join huge flocks of similar species that feed in pastures and marshes from autumn to spring. Their eating habits help control insects during nesting season.

Canada's twenty-one frog and nineteen salamander species inhabit the deciduous forests of southwest Ontario; all the country's eight freshwater turtle species are found in the southern parts of the province. Among them are the western and midland painted turtle and the Blanding's turtle, with a two-toned black and yellow neck. The smallest are the ten-centimetre musk, or stinkpot, turtle and the slightly larger spotted turtle. A less attractive species is the snapping turtle, lurking in lakes, marshes, stagnant ditches, and fish ponds from Saskatchewan to Nova Scotia. This spiny-shelled, prehistoric terrapin may grow to eighteen kilograms by devouring virtually anything it encounters—dead or alive.

The eastern box turtle, found in Canada only at Point Pelee National Park, was probably introduced. Like the box turtle, the wood turtle may wander some distance from water. Larger lakes and rivers are inhabited by soft-shelled and map turtles.

Larger water bodies are also the domain of the eastern Massasauga rattlesnake, found at Georgian Bay and in parts of Lakes Huron and Erie. It may grow to nearly a metre long and slither thirty kilometres inland in search of frogs and mice. Like other rattlesnakes, it has a venomous bite.

Much of the wildlife habitat of the Great Lakes region is protected within provincial and national parks. Long Point Provincial Park, on the northeast shore of Lake Erie, is part of a complex of sites for migrating songbirds and waterfowl and has a number of rare reptile and amphibian species.

Point Pelee National Park, 1,560 hectares at the southeast end of Lake Erie, is the southernmost point on the Canadian mainland, basking at a balmy latitude of forty-two degrees north. This park lies at a crossroad of two migratory fly-

ways and is internationally
known as one of North
America's premier birding areas.
At least one hundred species
nest here and more than three
hundred have been recorded,
including Louisiana water
thrushes, Carolina wrens, blue-
grey gnatcatchers, ruby-throated
hummingbirds, Lapland long-
spurs, short-billed dowitchers,
and parasitic jaegers. A 1987
study of bird-watching in the
park found that twenty thousand
birders spent a total of $5.4 mil-
lion to see Point Pelee's birds
that year.

Common loons can dive to sixty metres in
search of small fish. In their muscles
they have large amounts of myoglobin, a
respiratory pigment that allows them to
store oxygen for use underwater. The
loon was designed to swim, with legs so
far back that when it hauls itself from the
water it often flops forward on its breast.

The mallard is the largest dabbling duck and the most common of all Canadian waterfowl. The green-headed drake wears its colourful feathers year-round except in summer, when its eclipse plumage makes it appear similar to the hen.

The killdeer is one of the first spring migrants to return to eastern Canada, shortly after the first snow melts from the fields. Though a shorebird, it is more often seen on open uplands. During nesting it soaks its breast to cool eggs on hot days. It also pretends to have a broken wing to distract danger from its nest.

The bond between a cow moose and her calf is extremely strong. When
an outsider approaches the calf, the mother takes on a threatening
pose with bowed head, raised hair, downturned ears, and flared
nostrils. The calf trails its mother almost everywhere but will also
follow other moose and even people.

An avian mix of dunlins, dowitchers, sandpipers, and sanderlings takes to the air. These are among some five dozen shorebird species that occur in Canada. During spring and fall migrations, tens of thousands of shorebirds gather to feed on mud flats and estuaries throughout eastern Canada. They take to the air en masse when threatened by raptors or other dangers.

(Above) Red-shouldered hawks return repeatedly to the same breeding territories in southern Ontario and Quebec. They favour forests and woodlots near open fields, where they can forage for rodents, snakes, lizards, insects, and snails. Their numbers appear to be declining due to habitat loss.

(Opposite) Originally an Asian bird, the ring-necked pheasant was introduced to Canada, where it is distributed across the country. In breeding season this solitary male may preside over a group of females, which it abandons once its amorous desires are fulfilled.

(Above) Calling barred owls at night is a pleasant pastime of birders who listen for the distinctive who-cooks-for-you *call. Those who imitate the call invariably get a response if an owl is within hearing range. These birds are common in eastern Canada, where they occupy mixed coniferous and deciduous forests, wooded swamps, and river valleys.*

(Opposite) Whitetail deer does are doting mothers, usually hiding their newborns shortly after birth on the forest floor, where their spotted fur camouflages them. This doe likely has another fawn nearby, as they more often give birth to twins.

The tiny long-tailed weasel measures only fifty centimetres, including
its fifteen-centimetre black-tipped tail. Despite its diminutiveness, it is
a formidable foe of much larger prey, including adult snowshoe hares.
In winter this ferocious weasel is virtually identical to the ermine.

(Above) Timber wolves howl before a hunt. There is a great deal of pacing, whimpering and general restlessness before the hunt, led by a dominant pair, begins. The social hierarchy of wolves is unusual in the wild mammal world.

(Overleaf) An American robin eyes a patch of raspberries in the afternoon sun. Robins winter as far south as Bermuda or Guatemala, and their annual return to eastern Canada is considered an early sign of spring. The belief that robins catch worms by listening to the ground has been disproved by experiments showing that they hunt worms by sight.

Martens are inhabitants of coniferous forests. With widespread logging across Canada, marten populations, unable to survive in new deciduous forests, are declining. They are also curious animals, a trait which frequently draws them to traplines.

Giant snapping turtles rarely leave the water except to bury their eggs
on gravel or sandy shores with the help of powerful back legs. The
eggs are easy meals for skunks, raccoons, rats, and other predators.
Some of these turtles may grow to sixteen kilograms.

A hummingbird hovers by positioning its body at a forty-five-degree angle and rapidly moving its wings in a figure-eight pattern. Swivel-type joints at the shoulders allow it to create lift without momentum, making it appear stationary in the air. While hovering, its wings beat at least twenty times a second.

The muskrat, like the beaver, wears a coat of plush, waterproof fur
insulated by layers of trapped air. It swims with partially webbed feet,
steering with a tail that's flat at the end. Also like the beaver, the
muskrat builds lodges in which to house its family, but unlike its
aquatic cousin, it may dig its own riverbank burrow.

THE ATLANTIC COAST

The seabirds and marine life of the Canadian Atlantic are survivors of an era when unbridled exploitation pushed many animals to the edge of extinction. Some species—the sea mink, Labrador duck, great auk, Atlantic grey whale— did not endure.

Others, such as the creamy-white beluga whale, face a dubious future on Canada's official endangered-species list.

Perhaps the most visibly hunted Atlantic species was the harp seal. Each winter these Arctic seals swim five thousand kilometres to mate and bear their pups on the pack ice of the Labrador coast and the Gulf of St. Lawrence. It was here that hunters sought the pure white

These courting gannets are among more than forty thousand that nest at Bonaventure Island Provincial Park, off the eastern tip of Quebec's Gaspé Peninsula. This is the largest gannet colony in North America, luring thousands of birders who observe the nests by boating below the 120-metre-high cliffs.

pelts of newborn pups. This occupation was carried on for generations and one year—1831— nearly seven hundred thousand pups were taken by ten thousand sealers. More than 150 years later, Europe, the sealers' most lucrative market, reacted to animal-rights protests by banning the import of white harp-seal pelts as well as the shimmering blue pelts of hooded seal pups. In 1987 the Canadian government, while continuing to allow sealing, specifically prohibited the commercial hunting of "whitecoat" harp seals and "blueback" hooded seals. There are about 1.2 million harp seals and 300,000 hooded seals in Canadian waters today.

More stringent protection has been given to the beluga, whose numbers are seriously reduced. When explorer Jacques Cartier entered the St. Lawrence estuary in 1535 he saw a "species of fish" with "the body and head white as snow. . . a very large number in this river." They were hunted by natives and commercial whalers for meat, oil, and skins. Considered competition for fishermen, in the 1930s the Quebec government launched a beluga extermination program, paying bounties for dead whales. Today only a few hundred are left in the Gulf of St. Lawrence. Other small populations remain in the Arctic and they are occasionally seen in the Bay of Fundy.

Like the beluga, the slightly larger pilot whale is a toothed whale. Measuring four to six metres long, the so-called "pothead" has a blunt, bulbous head similar to that of the beluga. Atlantic pilot whales may gather in pods of five to three hundred during summer, but are most often seen in groups of twenty to fifty, near shore where they occasionally beach themselves. These small cetaceans share Canada's Atlantic seas with some of the world's largest creatures. The blue whale, as long as twenty-five metres, occurs in

Unlike its male partner, the female ring-necked pheasant lacks the colourful plumage and white throat ring. The hen, about a third smaller than the male, may evade its motherly duties by laying its eggs in a duck's nest.

these waters in summer and fall. It is listed as "rare" by the Committee on the Status of Endangered Wildlife in Canada (COSEWIC). Almost as large—up to twenty-three metres—and more common in the north Atlantic is the fin whale. The humpback whale, though it is considered "threatened" by COSEWIC, is the mainstay of an Atlantic whale-watching industry.

Three porpoise and dolphin species commonly seen in Canada are often found in the same waters as Atlantic whales. Harbour porpoises are particularly abundant in the Bay of Fundy and Gulf of St. Lawrence, areas frequented by belugas. White-beaked dolphins and Atlantic white-sided dolphins roam the seas between Cape Cod and Davis Strait.

Many Atlantic species, particularly seabirds, are protected today through habitat conservation. The 140-hectare Witless Bay Bird Sanctuary, thirty kilometres south of St. John's, Newfoundland, is at the centre of the North American breeding range for the Atlantic puffin. More than 225,000 of these clownlike birds breed on islands in the bay. Gull Island supports nesting populations of about 1.3 million Leach's storm-petrels and numerous black-legged kittiwakes and herring gulls. At least 100,000 Atlantic murres nest on nearby Great Island.

On the opposite side of the Island of Newfoundland, more than 175 bird species, including the peregrine falcon, gyrfalcon, golden plover, osprey, and whimbrel, inhabit Gros Morne National Park. This 195,000-hectare coastal wilderness is also home to a herd of Newfoundland caribou, one of the world's largest caribou subspecies.

South of Newfoundland, 101 hectares have been set aside on Margaree Island for colonies of great black-backed gulls, common terns, great cormorants,

Common murres roost on rock ledges high above the sea at the sixty-five-hectare Cape St. Mary's Bird Sanctuary in Newfoundland. These duck-sized seabirds crowd into nesting colonies, where each female lays a single egg on barren rock. The eggs are pear-shaped to help prevent them rolling off the cliffs, but evidence of unsuccessful hatching is spattered down the rock faces.

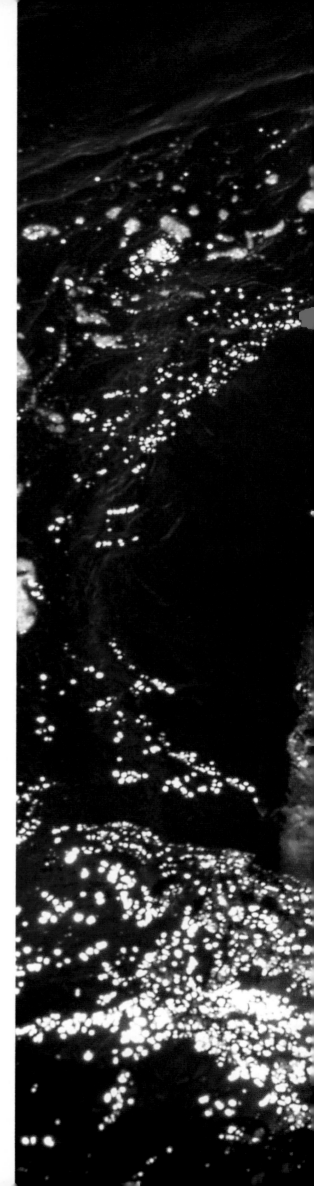

and black guillemots. Fundy
National Park in New Brunswick
is a twenty-one-thousand-hectare
refuge for 185 bird species
including great blue herons, bald
eagles, peregrine falcons, and
ospreys. Farther down the coast
some 245 species—eiders, ring-
necked ducks, blue- and green-
winged teals, black ducks, brant,
and more—find protection in the
eighty-one-hectare Grand Manan
Bird Sanctuary.

Among the more intriguing
visitors along Canada's Atlantic
shores are giant sea turtles.
Occasionally Atlantic ridley and
loggerhead turtles wash ashore,
and there are regular reports of
leatherback turtles becoming
tangled in fishnets. The leatherback is one of the world's largest
reptiles, weighing 550 kilograms
and measuring nearly two metres
in diameter. It travels from subtropical and tropical waters in
search of its favourite food, the
giant lion's mane jellyfish, a
common summer visitor to
North Atlantic waters.

*Humpbacks are the singers of the sea,
known for their eerie subaqueous vocal-
izations that reverberate through the
depths. These songs are produced only by
males in their southern breeding waters.
It's believed the songs may be an expres-
sion of dominance or aggression.*

Woodland caribou wander across the grasslands of Newfoundland's
Avalon Peninsula, site of a nine-hundred-square-kilometre wildlife
reserve. One side of their impressive antlers often grows larger than
the other. Caribou may ingest calcium by gnawing on discarded
antlers.

Royal terns breed in colonies with up to ten thousand nests, often sharing space with sandwich terns and laughing gulls. They feed mainly on crabs, squid, and shrimp, hovering above the sea before diving for their prey. Atlantic terns may winter as far away as South America.

(Above) A great blue heron stalks the shallows of Kouchibouguac National Park, a twenty-five-kilometre arc of sandbars, lagoons, and salt marshes off the central coast of New Brunswick. Herons wait patiently for a chance to spear small fish with their rapierlike bills.

(Opposite) A Canada goose and its goslings enjoy protection in Prince Edward Island National Park, a forty-kilometre stretch of shore on the island's north coast. This six-kilogram honker is the most pervasive North American goose, occupying summer and winter ranges across the entire continent.

(Above) Atlantic puffins, or sea parrots, survey their territories from Baccalieu Island, off the southeast coast of Newfoundland. These burrow nesters choose offshore islands as mating grounds to avoid attacks by dogs, cats, rats, foxes, and other terrestrial predators. Their numbers are declining, particularly near populated centres.

(Opposite) A great cormorant roosts on the rocks at Prince Edward Island's Cape Tryon, on the Gulf of St. Lawrence. With eyes adapted for both aerial and underwater vision, birds of this species in southeast Asia are trained to catch fish for fishermen.

(Overleaf) The kittiwake, a gull of the Arctic and east coasts, comes ashore only to reproduce. It builds a nest of grass, moss, and seaweed, anchored to steep rocks by mud. After a short stint ashore, it returns to the sea, where it can be heard calling its own name while following ships and schools of fish.

Distributed across most of Canada, the piping plover is becoming
scarce and now is officially endangered. There may be only four
thousand left. It was once seriously hunted and today it suffers from
habitat loss through development. Its nests, on sand or gravel beaches,
are sometimes crushed by vehicles

*The red fox, like the Arctic fox, curls into a ball to warm itself with its
bushy tail. The fox commonly known as the silver fox is actually a red
fox with silver-tipped fur.*

A lone female harp seal lies on the pack ice of the Atlantic coast.
Hunting the snow-white pups of these animals on the ice of the
Labrador coast and Gulf of St. Lawrence caused an international furor
in the 1980s. In 1987 the Canadian government banned the slaughter of
pups but continued to allow hunting of older seals.

The striped skunk rivals the porcupine for unusual weaponry. Its eye-watering, repugnant musk, however, is fired only in inescapable predicaments. Attackers are first warned by defensive displays before a skunk turns backside to the enemy and shoots.

Of Canada's twenty-two frog species, the wood frog is probably the most widespread. It is found coast to coast, including the Yukon and Northwest Territories. In the Yukon it occurs in forested river valleys above the Arctic circle.

Black guillemots inhabit Canada's Atlantic shores from the eastern Arctic south to Nova Scotia. During winter it stays offshore from breeding colonies if the water remains open, feeding on crustaceans, mollusks, and sea worms. It can dive to fifty metres and stay submerged up to seventy-five seconds.

PHOTO CREDITS

Paul Bailey p. 21
Michael Baytoff/First Light p. 136
Trevor Bonderud/First Light p. 10
Tim Christie pp. vi, 8, 29, 33, 55, 61, 66, 67, 80, 89, 106, 115, 119, 124
Graeme Ellis p. 18
Dawn Goss/First Light pp. 104, 105
Chris Harris/First Light pp. 64, 70
Richard Hartmier/First Light pp. 43, 56, 90
Stephen Homer/First Light pp. 134, 143, 144, 151
Thomas Kitchin/First Light pp. 5, 13, 14, 16, 22, 24, 25, 26, 34, 37, 45, 47, 50, 53, 58, 62, 68, 69, 72, 73, 78, 79, 81, 93, 98, 109, 110, 116, 117, 121, 129, 130, 149, 150, 152
Jerry Kobalenko/First Light p. 54
Robert Lankinen/First Light pp. 6, 23, 30, 51, 71, 103, 113, 126, 128
Scott Leslie/First Light pp. 100, 118, 127, 139
Peter McLeod/First Light pp. 94, 114, 120, 123
Brian Milne/First Light pp. 39, 42, 44, 46, 48, 74, 76, 82, 86, 95, 96, 97, 99, 102, 122
Pat Morrow p. 57
David Nunuk/First Light p. 28
Bruce Obee pp. 20, 31
G. Petersen/First Light pp. 138, 140
Robert Semeniuk/First Light p. 52
Steve Short/First Light p. 32
John Sylvester/First Light pp. 40, 75, 133, 141, 142, 146, 147
Ron Watts/First Light p. 2
Wayne Wegner/First Light p. 148
Darwin R. Wiggett/First Light pp. 85, 92

INDEX

Photographs in italics.